Just finished *Daddy C*
Heard, PGA. Great rea
ideas for parents and c
try a few ideas this com......

Nicole Weller, PGA
2013 National PGA Junior Leader

The Dedication in this book sets the tone, nothing short of amazing, and what follows in the book is just as great.

Kris Wilson, Founder and President, The Littlest Golfer, Inc.

Absolutely loved *Daddy-Caddy Off the Bag*! Such a fun read for juniors while guiding them on the mental aspects of the game! Favorite chapters are definitely "Mistakes are good" and "Mad is bad" Loved all the practice ideas and as a coach, I'll be using lots of them Well done again! Like I said before - Your books are going to help millions of juniors reach their true potential!

Michelle Holmes, Michelle Holmes School of Golf

Love this book! Great gift idea for golfers..or parents of golfers! Congrats, Rick!

Dr. Kim Guerrise

Daddy Caddy Off the Bag

Tournament Time!

Rick Heard, PGA

Published by ARD Publishing
Boca Raton, Florida
Printed in the United States of America

Text and cover design by Rick Heard
Illustrations by Rick Heard

 Like Daddy Caddy Off the Bag on facebook

ISBN-13: 978-0-9786717-5-4

For **Alex**

ACKNOWLEDGMENTS

Thanks to all of the junior golfers who were my friends and fellow-competitors growing up, especially including Wes Blumenauer, Carmen Rosamonda, Gordy Jones, Mike Jones, Patty Hayes, and Connie Chillemi. We all grew up on the golf course and taught each other everything we needed to know about golf and life (or so we thought at the time). Incredibly, Carmen, Mike and I went on to play college golf, and Connie and Patty both enjoyed successful careers on the LPGA Tour.

Thanks also to our parents and all of the other members of DeLand Country Club who tolerated a bunch of young limberbacks on and around their golf course.

Lastly, I am grateful for Pug Allen, Nick Chillemi, and Ken Leuenberger, my mentors and first PGA professionals.

INTRODUCTION

This is a book for young people who love golf.

I love golf too, and my hope is to inspire you to grow up to be a respectful, responsible golfer. It does not really matter whether you become a great golfer or just a golfer. I only want you to continue to love golf for the rest of your life.

I hope you will also use the lessons learned in golf to help you grow into a respectful, responsible person throughout your life.

The characters in this story are pretend, but they are based on my own experiences as a golf instructor and coach, as a parent and as a kid growing up on the golf course. Any similarities to actual people are coincidental, but some of the things in this story may have actually happened.

You may have heard of a book called

"Daddy Caddy on the Bag." That book is for your parents, to help them be better golf parents, and to help bring out the best in you on the golf course.

This book is for you. It is called "Daddy Caddy <u>Off</u> the Bag" because I hope it helps *you* bring out *your best* on the golf course. This is something you need to do on your own. Let it be your guide to independence on (and off) the golf course. With some luck, maybe it will even help you bring out the best in your parents, too!

Daddy Caddy
Off the Bag

Tournament Time!

CHAPTER ONE

"Never leave Never-Never Land."
– RICK HEARD

HAVE FUN

The diving board went "bonga-bonga-bonga" as Bobby bounced higher and higher into the air. It seemed like he could bounce forever, and it looked like the board would break each time his huge feet landed on it. Finally, he launched into space, did a half flip, and landed with a gigantic splash that covered Isabella's sleeping body with five gallons of cold pool

Bobby's surprise for Isabella.

water. End of poolside nap for her.

"Ahhhhhh!" she screamed as she jumped up in surprise. "Just for that, I'll birdie the last hole again to beat you, just like this morning!"

Nothing made Bobby madder than losing, especially to someone half his size. Especially to a girl. Especially to Isabella. But that is how their matches often went.

He would blast a drive 250 yards or more. She would follow with a controlled tee shot in the center of the fairway. Every time. Then the center of the green. Every time. Then the center of the hole. Almost every time. At least it seemed that way. It drove him crazy, but he always came back for more.

As much as he hated losing, Bobby loved competing. It was so much fun to make up new games, new challenges, and new matches with Isabella or any of the other kids who hung around the golf course with him.

It was even more fun to compete in junior golf tournaments, and the next one was coming up in only a week. Bobby was entered in the tournament, and so was Isabella. They both wanted to practice hard this week to get ready.

Now that he was thirteen years old, Bobby often felt too old to play with some of the younger kids. His biggest weakness was his temper, and the others loved to take advantage of that fault. Bobby knew that he needed to let go of his bad shots and not let them bother him, but it seemed almost impossible to do, especially when it counted in tournaments. He promised himself that this weekend's event would be different.

The youngest of Bobby's golf friends was Ben. Only eight, Ben could keep up with Bobby around the greens, and was tough to beat when he played from the 8-year old tees. His strength was his confidence, and he felt he could pull off almost any shot at any time. Ben was also practicing for the upcoming tournament.

Ten years old, easygoing and quiet, Sam

was thoughtful and careful, always thinking through his options before trying a shot. He sometimes took too long to play, causing the others to yell "while we're young!" Even though his golf skills were not as sharp as the others, he always stayed cool as a cucumber and often came out on top. Sam was the best putter of the group, but he felt he wasn't ready to play in tournaments yet. Even so, he always hung around with the other kids and practiced with them.

Also ten, Nicole was almost as tall as Bobby and could hit the ball almost as far with her lightning-fast swing and tour tempo. Never the one to play it safe, Nicole found great fun in going for broke, hitting her driver "off the deck," and didn't mind if she pulled off the unlikely shot only half the time. She was also signed up for this weekend's big event and was doing her best to get ready.

Then there was Isabella. Like Bobby, Ben, and Nicole, she was prepping for this weekend's tournament. One year younger than Bobby. Half his size. Quiet. Patient, yet strong-willed. Nothing rattled her (except maybe having gallons of cold pool water splashed on her while she slept on the lounge chair).

"I'll get you, Bobby!" she repeated. "Go get your clubs and meet me at the range."

At the sound of this challenge, the others nearly flew out of the pool and into their locker rooms to get back into their golf clothes. They all loved a challenge on the range. Whether it was hitting the picker, ricocheting balls off the tall range fence pole, bouncing a ball into the 100-yard sign, or pitching over the practice bunker, they could do it all day. And, that is what they did, day after day, all summer long.

Up at dawn. Quick breakfast (thanks, mom). Golf clothes on. Out the door and to the putting green. Over to the range, then on the first tee for whatever crazy game they invented for the day. Match play. Stroke play.

Alternate shot. Best shot scramble. Worst shot scramble. One-club holes. Opposite side holes (Ben, the lefty, had to play righty while everyone else played lefty). Birdie-fest from the 100-yard marker. Stableford points. Mulligans. Lift, clean, and place. Bad lies on purpose. Cross country. There seemed to be no end, and the more creative they got, the more fun they had.

Sure, every now and then they played "real" golf, and they were always ready for a junior tournament, but they had the most fun creating their own "Masters," with their own rules, and laughing their way around the course.

That is how it had been this morning. Bobby, Isabella, and Ben had played nine holes, but counted them as eighteen holes using their favorite scoring system that they called "321." It went like this: Count the first hole three times. Count holes two through four only once each. Count holes five, six and seven twice each. And, count holes eight and nine three times each.

They loved this weird scoring because it made them really focus on starting well and finishing strong, and it had produced many fantastic, come from behind finishes over the summer.

Today, Isabella had birdied the ninth, and since it was counted three times, she had made up three strokes against Bobby's par to beat him by one, 82 to 83.

They usually hit the pool after the morning game and grabbed a sandwich at the snack bar. Then, like today, it was back to the putting green, range, or course for more fun. This time they were luckier than usual, because Mike, the PGA pro, was just finishing up a lesson and saw them coming to the range, full of smack talk and ready to rumble – golf style.

Never at a loss for fun practice ideas, Mike quickly grabbed an empty golf club set box from his cart, got out his marking pens, and waited. "Okay, Ben," he said as the youngest of the kids walked up. "Take this pen and draw a big face on the side of this box. It's time for a game of what I call Wham-Box."

"Hey, don't you kids have a big tournament this weekend?" Mike asked.

"Ben, Nicole, Isabella, and I do," replied Bobby. "Sam is sitting this one out."

"Well, this game might just help you guys hit trouble shots, in case you happen to need one," Mike explained.

'Hmm… whose face should I draw," muttered Ben as he did his best to draw a funny face on the box. The finished product wasn't too bad, with glasses and all. In fact, it looked a lot like Bobby, except for the added mustache Ben decided it needed.

"Now, just wait a moment," said Mike, as he took the box and ran 30 yards out onto the range. He stood the box upright, dumped about 20 range balls inside to keep it from falling over, closed the top, and ran back. "To your stations, kids," he yelled, then "three, two, one... FIRE!"

That box was never the same again, and neither were the knock-down, punch trouble shot skills of five golf friends who pelted it with balls that day. Their sides splitting with laughter, they learned more about how to control their golf balls playing "wham-box" than anyone (except Mike) could have imagined. And, they had so much fun that they couldn't wait to come back the next day.

CHAPTER TWO

"If you don't know where you are, you will never get to where you want to go."
– RICK HEARD

WHERE ARE YOU?

Back at the pool, the five friends relaxed and had a few more laughs about "wham-box" and how they had destroyed Ben's drawing. "That sure was a blast," said Sam.

"Absolutely," chimed in Nicole. "But that shot was not easy for me. I kept hitting the ball too high no matter what club I used."

"My shots almost always hooked and missed to the left," added Bobby. "I started to get the hang of it, but it's a hard shot for me."

"Not me," Ben insisted. "I've got that shot. But it's a good thing we weren't trying to hit into that old wading pool Coach Mike had us try last week. That shot was impossible."

"No way, that was a piece of cake," said Isabella. "I loved that wading pool shot, but 'wham-box' was tough for me too. Hey, wait a minute! Isn't it strange that we all have different strengths? Some shots are hard for me, but easy for you guys."

At that, Nicole piped up. "Coach Mike says that all golfers have some things they do well, and some things they don't do so well."

"Yeah," added Ben, "my dad is always keeping track of how I play in tournaments, and he probably knows my game better than I do."

"Hmm, that's not good," Nicole replied.

"Coach Mike says we each need to know our own games. Where we do well, our most reliable shots, and where we need to improve. Your dad won't be caddying for you forever."

"Well, how are we supposed to do it?" asked Ben. "I just play and don't really worry about stuff like that."

Bobby jumped in. "Relax, dude. It isn't hard. You just have to keep track of a few things like hitting fairways and greens, scrambling, and putting, and stuff like that. I do it all of the time."

"You do?" asked Ben. "I've never seen you do anything like that.

"That's because I just make a few marks on my scorecard. Then when I get home, I think about my round and enter some stats in a spreadsheet on my computer. It's simple. That way, I know where I am and what I need to work on in practice."

"Take this morning, for example," continued Bobby, sitting up in his lounge chair. "I hit almost every fairway, but my approach shots were awful. I kept missing the green to the left. Just like I did trying to hit that box. Then, my chipping was pretty good, but I missed a whole bunch of short par putts."

"Yeah," said Isabella. "And I three-putted almost every time I was more than 20 feet away."

Ben thought about his last round. "Well, I did have a bunch of shots from 30-40 yards, and I didn't get any of them close to the hole. And my putting was awful too. I guess my dad knows all of that, but maybe I need to pay more attention."

Sam couldn't resist any more. "Well, guys, I have the secret to understanding your own golf game. And, if someone would just go to that snack bar and bring me an ice cream sandwich, I might just tell you what it is."

Hearing that, the other four jumped up, grabbed Sam, and tossed him into the pool.

Scorecard stats are easy to do!

"Hahaha," they all laughed. "You can get your own ice cream sandwich. And then you can still tell us your silly secret. And off to the snack bar they all ran.

Dried off again and feeling the ice cream sandwich in his belly, Sam continued. "All right. It's no big secret, anyway. Coach Mike plans to help all of us work on it. Like Bobby said, it is simple. You just use a special 'golf stats' scorecard to help keep track of things."

"This still sounds complicated," said Ben.

Sam went on. "Well, it is actually pretty simple if you write things down when they happen. It's a lot harder if you wait until after your round to do it. You don't even need a special scorecard. You can use a regular course scorecard and mark your stats on it."

"That's right," said Bobby as he reached into his backpack. "That's how I do it. Here, I'll show you. This is my card from this morning."

16

Hole	1	2	3	4	5	6	7
Yards	475	160	390	410	375	170	525
Par	5	3	4	4	4	3	5
1ˢᵗ Shot	(D)	6	D	(D)	(3W)	(4)	D
2ⁿᵈ Shot	3W		7	5	8		5W
3ʳᵈ Shot	SW						(9)
Pitch/Chip		SW P	(8 C)	SW C	SW B		
Putts	(2)	2	1	3	2	(2)	(1)
Score	5	4	4	6	5	3	4

Sample Scorecard Stat Tracker Instructions

Write the initials of the club used for your 1ˢᵗ, 2ⁿᵈ, and 3ʳᵈ full shots. D=Driver, 3W=3-wood, 6=6-iron, SW=sand wedge, etc.

Write the initials of the club used for pitching, chipping, or bunkers. SWP is a pitch. SWC is a chip. SWB is a bunker shot.

Circle any shot that you are happy with, such as hit the fairway.

Circle the Putts box if you are on the green in regulation.

Add the "good shot" circles at the end to get a total count. Add the putt circles to get a total number of greens hit in regulation.

"See," continued Bobby as he pointed to his scorecard. "I just write in what happened on each shot. You know, what club I used and all. Then, if I hit a good shot, I draw a circle around it."

"What do you mean by good shot?" asked Nicole.

"It could be any shot where you are happy with the result. For me, I circle my tee shots, long second shots, or layups when I hit the fairway. For an approach shot, it is when I hit the green. If I chip it close like I did on number three, I circle those too."

"What about those other circles around the number of putts?"

"Those are for when I hit the green in regulation. You know, when I'm on the green in one on a par 3, two on a par 4, or on in three on a par 5."

"Looks easy enough," agreed Ben.

"But then, you have to take the card home with you and think about what happened during your round," Sam replied.

Bobby went on. "Right. That's why the

card is in my backpack. I keep my stats from every round. I must have hundreds of stats. I put them into the spreadsheet, then I look at how I'm doing. Like I said, lately too many of my approach shots have been missing the greens. Next time we practice, I'm gonna really work on those shots."

Ben thought for a moment. "I think I know what my stats would show. I guess I should work a lot harder on my putting. My long putts aren't getting close enough, and those four to five footers are almost always for par. I hate to practice them, and I guess it shows in my game."

"But maybe your putting isn't the problem," said Sam. "Maybe you aren't hitting your approach shots close enough to the hole."

"Well, maybe you are right. I do usually have lots of long putts. If I had my stats I would know for sure."

Nicole pitched in. "Coach Mike told me

that everyone loves to practice what they are already good at. And they hate to practice what they really need. That's why he keeps coming up with all of those crazy games for us to play. They are really practice drills, but at least he makes them more fun to do."

"Right," Sam added thoughtfully. "And keeping these stats helps us figure out where we are, so we know what we need to work on. Otherwise, we would probably keep practicing the wrong things."

"Well I really want to keep getting better," replied Ben. "Especially with the tournament coming up. I kind of know what I need to do now, but it would sure help to have my stats. Then I could really see when and where my game is improving. And, it would be fun for me to do it myself and impress my dad."

"Yeah," agreed Nicole. "And I'd like to impress my mom."

CHAPTER THREE

"If you can dream it, you can do it."
— **Walt Disney**

Sam's phone buzzed with a text from his mom. "Hey guys," he yelled. "I've got to be home by six. We have time for one quick game of Last One Standing, if you think you can beat me!"

"We don't think we can beat you," Isabella retorted. "We KNOW we can beat you!"

"Let's go," they all shouted together, and they picked up their towels and hurried to the locker rooms to change.

The five friends loved to play Last One Standing, and Sam was usually the winner. The game involved everyone putting their ball to a string stretched across the green. On each turn, the person whose ball was farthest from the string would be eliminated. The winner was the last one remaining after the final turn.

Sam had the uncanny ability to stop his ball right next to the string, and he did it almost all of the time. At least, it seemed that way to the others. He even kept a roll of string in his golf bag for just these occasions, and he was always ready to play his favorite putting game. His distance control skills really helped him on the golf course. He was able to two-putt from almost anywhere, and he almost always left his ball within a few feet from the hole.

First to be dressed, Sam ran from the locker room to the putting green and set up the string. The others were not far behind him. Sam paused for a moment.

"I've been thinking," Sam said when everyone was together on the green. "Remember yesterday when we were all talking about playing golf in high school and college? I don't know about you guys, but I have been thinking about that a lot."

"I know I'm only ten," he continued. "But I can really see myself playing for some big college team some day."

"Yeah," joked Nicole. "Especially if the team plays its matches on the putting green!"

"Hey! That's not fair," Sam shot back. "The rest of my game is okay. Putting just happens to be one of my strengths, like Coach Mike says. He told me that I needed to dream."

"I dream every night," laughed Bobby.

"Not that kind of dream. Coach Mike was talking about my goals. He said we all need to think about where we want to be someday. He even asked me to write my goals and dreams on paper."

"What about the game?" asked Isabella. "Aren't we going to play Last One Standing? Or are we just going to stand around dreaming?"

Just then, Mike, who had been watching all of this from the pro shop, walked over to the putting green to act as the Last One Standing judge.

"What's up, guys?" he asked. "Ready to play?"

"Yeah, but Sam is too busy dreaming," Bobby replied.

Sam looked annoyed. "I was just telling them what you said about goals and stuff," he said.

Mike intervened. "Well, there may be nothing more important than dreaming about your future. If you don't know where you want to go, you are lost. Tell you what. Let's get this game started, and when each of you is eliminated, you will have to tell the rest of us something about your dreams and goals. And,

I want to you to tell us one thing that you would like to accomplish right now. Okay, let's get going."

And with that, Mike called everyone to the starting line, about 25 feet away from the string. "Three, two, one... PUTT!" he yelled. Five balls rolled toward the string, and Mike pointed to Bobby.

"All right, all right. This game isn't fair," Bobby complained. He hated to be the first one out. "Here goes. I love golf, and I dream of playing it forever with my friends and family. And I dream of winning this crazy game some day."

"Very cool," Mike said. "Not everyone will be a tour pro. In fact, professional golf is a really tough life, and only a small number of great players ever make it that far. But everyone can enjoy golf for the rest of their lives. It will be a great way for you to meet friends and do business whether you are a great player or not."

"How about for right now?" Mike asked. "What golf goal would you like to accomplish now?"

"Well, I guess I'd like to stop getting so mad at myself and be able to handle making mistakes."

"Fantastic," Mike replied. "We all make mistakes, and we need to find a way to put them behind us and move on. Okay, ready? Three, two, one… PUTT!"

Four balls rolled toward the string.

Nicole groaned as Mike pointed to her. Her ball was only about a foot from the string, but this time, Sam, Isabella, and Ben were each closer. "For now, I'd like to play smarter, and for the future, I dream of getting a college golf scholarship."

Mike smiled as he said "Awesome. Getting a college scholarship is a really big goal, and it can save your family thousands of dollars on college costs. Its lucky for you and Isabella that there are more scholarships for girls than there are for boys. And as good as you are already, you will have a great chance of getting one if you keep working on your game. Now let's keep going. Three, two, one… PUTT!"

Three balls rolled toward the string.

Isabella's stopped right next to the string – a "leaner." Ben's came up just inches away. Perhaps the thought of a scholarship had Sam dreaming at the wrong time, because Sam's ball shot two feet past the string, and Mike pointed to him.

"Well, for now, I'd like to learn to play faster and not over-think my shots. For the future, you know my goal is to play in college, too," Sam said. "But not just anywhere. My dream is to play for the Florida Gators."

"Hey, I played for them," Mike said. "I didn't get a scholarship, but I made the team anyway."

"What do you mean?" Sam asked.

"Not everyone on a college team gets a scholarship. A lucky few get some financial help, but many of the team members are there because they love golf and they are good enough to make it through qualifying. Getting a scholarship is really difficult, and it requires great grades and great golf ability."

"Great grades?" groaned Ben. "Why does that matter?"

"Because schools won't pay for you to play golf for them if you can't keep up with the academic work. And, if you did get a scholarship, you would have to keep making good grades in order to keep it. Okay, ready for the final round? Three, two, one... PUTT!"

Two balls rolled toward the string.

Maybe it was the excitement of the final putt. Perhaps he just lost his focus for a moment. Ben's ball stopped three feet short of the string, and Isabella let out a scream.

"Finally," she yelled.

Mike pointed to Ben.

"I want to be a better putter, and I dream

Isabella's dream.

of playing on the PGA Tour," he said.

"Well I want to improve my short game, and I dream of playing on the LPGA Tour," echoed Isabella.

Mike thought for a moment and said "Wow. Those are great dreams. Did you know that each year, thousands of golfers try to make it on Tour? They go through what we call Tour School, but it really isn't school. It is a series of tournaments, and only the top players make it through. Tour School is a lot like Last One Standing. There are four tournaments, called stages."

Mike continued. "Hundreds of players make it to the pre-qualifying stage, but only about 75 make it to the next stage. By the final stage, only about 50 players get to play on the Web.com Tour for the next year. If they do well there, they will qualify for the PGA Tour for the following year."

"It works the same for the LPGA Tour, but with three stages. The top players from the final stage get to play on the LPGA Tour for the next year."

"The great thing about dreams," Mike went on, "is that anything is possible. It all starts with a dream, and if you can dream it, you can do it. The other great thing about dreams is that they can grow and change when you want them to. Dreams provide the motivation to set goals. Goals are like a map that leads to your dream, and they give you something to work for, like a challenge. And, I know you all love a challenge!"

"Now here is a project for each of you," Mike added. "Take a minute or two and write your dreams down on paper. Then, write down those "right now" goals that can help you get closer to your dream. Something magical seems to happen when we write things on paper, and it will really help your dreams come true. Now I'm ready to close up the pro shop, so you guys get on home, okay?"

And with that, five young golfers each

headed home with their heads full of thoughts and dreams of the future. What would it take to make their dreams come true?

CHAPTER FOUR

"Practice doesn't make perfect. Perfect practice makes perfect."

– Vince Lombardi

PRACTICE, PRACTICE, PRACTICE

Only four days remained until the tournament. Twice each week the course was closed to junior golfers until noon. Tuesday was Ladies Day, and Wednesday morning was reserved for the Men's Association.

Today was Tuesday.

Ben was not happy.

On Tuesdays and Wednesdays, Ben and his friends couldn't tee off until after lunch, so they usually practiced in the morning. He loved to play golf but hated to practice. He especially hated to practice the shots that were the hardest for him, like four-foot putts and lagging the ball up close to the hole from far away so he could avoid those four footers. He would much rather just hit full shots on the range, even though the short game shots were much more important to his scores.

Nicole, however, loved to practice the scoring shots. Ben had just arrived at the course, hoping to skip off to the range to hit drivers, when up walked Nicole.

"Hey, Ben," she called. "How about a game of Threes?" Ben had to admit that, if he was forced to practice his putting, playing Threes was the most fun game.

"Well, I wanted to go to the range, but I

guess this will help me be a better putter. Okay, you're on," he replied.

Threes was a simple game the kids had made up one steamy afternoon. Each player used three balls and putted each one from a starting point into a designated hole on the putting green. They took turns choosing the starting point and the target hole.

If a ball was holed in one putt, it earned one credit that could be used to pay for a three-putt. If a ball was holed in two putts, no problem. If a ball was three-putted, the player had two ways to pay for the error. They could use a one-putt credit as payment for the three-putt. If the player had no one-putt credits, they had to do three push-ups. The payment had to be made immediately, and once a one-putt credit was used to pay for a three-putt, it was no longer usable for future three-putts.

Ben didn't like three-putting, and he really didn't like doing push-ups. But, he certainly didn't mind if Nicole had to do a few of them.

"At least we will get both our muscles and our putting in better shape," he continued.

Nicole took charge. "Let's start from here and putt to that hole," she directed, and off they went.

An hour later and feeling exhausted after way too many push-ups, Ben still wasn't happy. Just as they were about ready to take a break, Isabella showed up.

"Hi guys. Getting some exercise this morning, Ben?" She knew he had been doing a few extra push-ups by the pieces of cut grass stuck to his knees. "Where are Sam and Bobby?"

Nicole spoke up. "Oh, I think Bobby had an orthodontist appointment. He told me last night that he wouldn't be around this morning, and we haven't seen Sam."

Isabella went on. "Well, I promised Coach Mike that I would practice my short game today. Anyone want to play Scrambled Eggs?"

Ben needed a rest. "I think Nicole and I are

going to take a break and grab a snack. We've been playing Threes for hours."

"It only seems like that to you," Nicole corrected. "Let's go to the pro shop."

Just then, all 71 pounds of Sam struggled up to the practice green, looking like he was losing a battle with his golf bag. Sam usually used his three-wheel push cart, but he had left it in his dad's car last night. Sam's dad, and his beloved cart, were at work. Sam and his monster 40 pound golf bag were here.

"Did you say Scrambled Eggs? I've already had breakfast," he joked. As usual, no one laughed. "Actually, I'm in," Sam offered. He loved practicing his short game and he had invented Scrambled Eggs. Now it was his favorite chipping game. He and Isabella each grabbed three balls, made sure they were marked for identification, and headed to the chipping green.

Scrambled Eggs was simple and fun, and really tested their short game and putting skills.

They would take turns choosing a starting location around the chipping green. Each player would hit three balls from that spot, using the club of their choice.

The opponent would then decide which of the player's three shots would count, and the player's other two balls were picked up and moved to that location. This process would continue until each player had holed all three balls. The first player to win three times was the champion.

Sometimes they made the game easier by letting each player choose which of their own shots to use.

An hour later, Isabella was beaming. "I've got to hand it to you, Sam," Isabella crowed as she holed a five-footer for her third win. "This is a great game, and it is an honor to defeat its creator!"

Sam managed a groan. "Thanks a lot. Now let's find Ben and Nicole and go pound some range balls."

Sometimes, like this morning, the friends practiced shots that were all different. The game of Threes was a lot like playing real golf, since the challenge was to two-putt from anywhere, and the putt was different each time. Scrambled Eggs was similar. The challenge was to get "up and down" from all kinds of different situations, limited only by their imaginations. Golf is like that.

Coach Mike loved these games since each one gave the kids a few tries from each location. That way they could learn from their experience and improve each time.

When the four arrived at the range, they were surprised to find Bobby and Coach Mike there. "Hey Bobby, what's up?" asked Sam. "We thought you were at the orthodontist."

"I was, but it didn't take too long. Just a cleaning and some adjustments to my braces to fix a broken wire. Believe your mom when she tells you not to chew gum when wearing braces! I just got here, and Coach Mike said something about a new practice game he wants us to try."

"Cool," said Isabella. "What is it, Coach Mike?"

"Well," he replied. "I call it the Scorecard Race. It's for hitting full shots to a target, and it is a great way to prep for a big tournament."

"Can we all play?" asked Ben.

"Sure. Here is how it goes. First, take a regular scorecard and write your names on each line, like normal. Then, agree on a target that everyone can reach, like that 100 yard sign on the range."

"Then, we have to get a bit creative and imagine that the sign is sitting in the middle of a green. So, ten yards around the sign would be the edges of the green. The object is to land your ball on that imaginary green."

"Sounds simple enough," said Isabella.

"It is simple," continued Mike. "With a catch. You guys will take turns hitting to the imaginary green. The first time you land on the green, put a mark in the scorecard box for hole number one. Each time your ball lands on the green, you put a mark on your scorecard in the box for the next hole. If you miss the green, no mark."

"Still sounds easy," said Ben.

Mike finished the instructions. "Here's the catch. The first person to put a mark in all nine boxes for the front nine of the scorecard is the winner."

"But that wouldn't be fair, since whoever goes first would have the advantage," complained Nicole.

"Well, the game doesn't end until each player has had the same number of turns," explained Mike. "So it is fair. And, as with real golf, there is a lot of pressure to hit great shots. Best of all, you will get really good at concentrating and focusing on your target. Now I've got to go in and finish up this morning's ladies association tournament," and off he drove.

"Okay, let's give it a try," the five friends all agreed.

"But, let's warm up a bit first," said Isabella, always sounding like someone's mother.

Scorecard Race proved to be just like most of the games they played. It came down to the wire. After five tries, Ben had taken the early lead, hitting the green each time. Sam, Bobby and Nicole had each missed once. Isabella had missed twice.

Mike had suggested that each person act as the judge for their own shots.

"That is like golf," he had said. "You are responsible for your own score. Sometimes, only you will know if a rule has been broken. It is up to you to have integrity and to be honest. If you hit your shot well and you think it would be on the imaginary green, then it counts. If there is a difference of opinion, the other four of you will act as the 'rules committee,' and will make a final decision as a group. You will have to live with that decision."

Ben missed the green with his next two shots, then hit three more in a row. Sam, Bobby and Nicole each missed one more and hit four. Isabella drilled the next five shots.

After ten tries, they each had missed only two shots, and everyone had marked the first eight boxes. Only one more to go.

Nicole went first, and nailed it. "All right!" she yelled as she did her best fist pump.

"Not so fast, girlfriend," Isabella reminded her. "Remember what Coach Mike said. We each get the same number of turns. Since you went first, we all get one more shot."

Nicole had forgotten. "Oops! You're right. But, don't let the pressure get to you!"

Next to hit, Sam skipped his usual slow pre-shot routine and rushed his swing. The result was predictable: a block to the right that missed the green. "Arrrrgh!" he groaned. "I knew we should have stayed on the putting green."

Bobby hadn't thought about his swing mechanics until now. But, the extra pressure of knowing he had to hit the green made him think about the grip change Coach Mike had suggested a few days ago. He hadn't hit a big hook this morning... until now. "Aaaaaah!" he cried.

Isabella was next, and more than anything, she wanted to force Nicole to a playoff. Last week, in a tournament, Isabella had needed to par the final hole to break 40. Just at the wrong time, her swing tempo had gotten too quick and she had chunked her final approach, leaving with a bogey. It happened again. "Noooooo!" she wailed.

It was up to Ben for the final shot. "Keep your head steady," suggested Nicole.

"Don't worry, I will. Nothing bothers me," replied Ben, as he took a deep breath, exhaled slowly and fired his 7-iron right at the 100 yard marker, missing it by inches. "Oh, yeah!" he yelled and he and Nicole were left to play off.

She had won the morning game of Threes, with Ben getting the most push-up exercise. In the playoff, Nicole would go first. If she missed the green and Ben hit it, he would win. If she hit it and Ben missed, she would win. If they both missed, they would keep going.

She hit the green.

He hit the green.

She missed the green.

He missed the green.

She hit the green.

He hit the green.

She missed.

He didn't.

Now Ben was happy.

"Come on, I'll buy you a lemonade," he offered to Nicole, as they all headed to the clubhouse for lunch.

CHAPTER FIVE

*"Real integrity is doing the right thing,
knowing that nobody's going to know
whether you did it or not."*

— Oprah Winfrey

WHO ARE YOU?

Mike had just finished announcing the winners of the ladies association Tuesday stableford event, and he smiled when he saw the five friends walk into the clubhouse for lunch.

"Mind if I join you?" he asked. He knew they loved sharing stories as much as he enjoyed spending time with them.

"Not at all," replied Sam, and they all sat down full of chatter about the Scorecard Race playoff.

"Who won the race?" Mike asked.

"Ben got me in a playoff," replied Nicole. "But I won the morning game of Threes."

"And I won Scrambled Eggs," boasted Isabella.

Mike cautioned them. "Sounds like you are all winners," he said. "Those are great practice games, and you all improved a bit today."

Ben changed the subject. "Coach Mike, I have a rules question."

"Okay. Fire away."

"What happens if someone's ball goes into a water hazard and no one is sure where it went in? A couple of weeks ago, this other kid sliced his tee shot into the water. I didn't see exactly where it went, but he wanted to drop way ahead up the fairway, in line with where it splashed. I was sure it didn't cross the hazard line up there, but I couldn't prove it."

"So what ended up happening?" Mike asked.

"Well, he won the argument and dropped up there, then reached the green and sunk his putt for a birdie. He never could have done that from where I thought his ball went into the hazard."

"This raises a whole bunch of interesting points," Mike offered. "First, everyone in the group should have watched the ball flight from the tee. That way everyone could agree on where it crossed by lining it up with a red stake, a bush, or some other marker. Things always look different when you walk up to the spot than they did from the tee."

Mike saw this as an opportunity to discuss a deeper subject and forged ahead. "But the more important topic is personal integrity and playing by the rules. If we were playing Monopoly and I was about to land on your property, would it be okay if I moved one extra space as long as no one was looking?"

"No way," Bobby said. "That would be cheating."

"What if I didn't know the rules?" Mike asked.

"Then you should ask," continued Bobby. "You still have to play by the rules, even if you don't know them."

"But what if no one knew I did it?" Mike continued.

"You would know it," Isabella joined in. "You would know that you cheated, and that's bad enough. Like my dad says, it will catch up with you someday and everyone will know. Then, people will wonder about everything you have ever done."

"Right," Sam added. My mom says that if you have integrity, nothing else matters. And if you don't have integrity, nothing else matters."

"I'm not sure what 'integrity' is," said Ben.

"Integrity is doing the right thing even when no one else would know if you didn't," Mike explained. "Without integrity, golf wouldn't be much fun, and the rules would be meaningless. Golfers are expected to know the rules of the game and to follow them without other people having to check."

Mike continued. "Here's an example. A few years ago, I was playing in a PGA tournament. On the 14th hole, my ball was just off the green, about 40 feet from the hole, and I decided to use my putter. Just as I took my backswing, my ball rolled about half an inch. I couldn't stop my swing, and I hit the putt anyway. No one else saw it, since they were far away. But I saw it."

"What did you do?" asked Nicole.

"What should I have done?" asked Mike.

"Is that even a penalty?" asked Ben.

Bobby stepped in. "I'll try this one. I think you should have added a two-stroke penalty for hitting a moving ball."

"No," said Isabella. "You need to check the rules. It is was one-stroke penalty, since his ball moved and he kept swinging and hit the ball. But, if he had stopped his swing and not moved his ball back to where it had been, it would have been a two-stroke penalty."

Sam said "that's right. And if he had moved it back, it would only be a one-stroke penalty."

"A-plus for Isabella and Sam," Mike complimented. "The rules of golf can be pretty complicated, and many strange situations can happen. People's golf balls have ended up in some very interesting places, but there are always rules to help figure out what to do. That is really the purpose of the rules of golf. They help us finish each hole, even if we lose our ball or are unable to hit it from some bad place. And, the rules keep the game fair for everyone. Do you each have a rules book in your golf bag?"

Four hands went up.

Bobby's head went down.

"Hmmm. Why not, Bobby?" Mike asked.

"Well, I had one, but it got wet in the rain a few weeks ago, and I forgot to get a new one."

"Stop by the pro shop later and I'll take care of you," Mike offered. "As much as you guys play, you all need to have a rules book in your bag all of the time. And, you need to read it. It really isn't so bad. There are only 34 rules. Oh, and keep the rules book inside a plastic baggie so it won't get wet."

Mike kept going. "Think about the other games you all play, at home, at school, or anywhere. You know the rules, and you expect everyone to play by them. If they didn't, you wouldn't want to play. Golf is the only sport where the players are their own referees. That is one of the great things that makes golf so special."

Mike didn't really like lecturing, but he was on a roll. "Golf places all of us in some difficult situations from time to time, and it is up to us to know what to do. And, to do the right thing even if you are all alone. Doing the right thing is a big part of who you are. It is a measure of your honesty and integrity, and of what other people will think of you and whether they will trust you."

"When it comes to the rules of golf, you all have a few important responsibilities. Who can name one?"

"Like you said, to know them," offered Ben.

"And to follow them," added Bobby.

"What about other golfers?" asked Nicole. "Don't we need to make sure they follow the rules too?"

"Right," Mike interjected. "That is called protecting the field. It wouldn't be fair to everyone else if you allowed someone to break a rule."

Sam thought for a moment, then spoke. "This rules stuff is a lot more important than I ever thought. I'll bet I could sometimes even save a stroke or two if I knew the rules better."

"Great observation, Sam," Mike said. "What about you, Isabella?"

"Well, I'm thinking that knowing the rules

and following them is a way that we can all show that we are honest and have integrity. I sure want my friends to trust me, and I want to trust them too. Golf really has a way of letting us find out what kind of person we are."

"And, what kind of person you will become as you grow older," finished Mike.

Coming through!

CHAPTER SIX

"Like the golf swing, character is something that is best developed from the time a person is very young."
– Ben Hogan

ETI-WHAT?

After lunch, they usually relaxed for a while before going back out into the heat for more practice or to play nine holes. Today was no exception.

"Who's up for some ping-pong?" Bobby asked, knowing the answer.

Mrs. Thompson and Mrs. Goldman had chosen the wrong time to stand in the middle of the dining room, chatting about plans for this evening's dinner-dance. Fortunately, they looked up just in time to avoid being trampled by a herd of five young golfers who jumped up from the table and dashed across the dining room to the stairs. From the far corner of the room, Mike gave a disapproving look.

Down in the game room, he had a few words for the kids. "Hey, guys. What was that all about? You know that is unacceptable behavior in the clubhouse. You are lucky that the adults allow kids to eat up there, but that could change if you don't act appropriately. Now I want you to go back upstairs and apologize to those ladies. Then come back down and let's talk about etiquette."

Sheepishly, five pairs of shoes climbed the stairs to the dining room, found Mrs. Thompson and Mrs. Goldman, and apologized.

"We're really sorry," offered Isabella, staring at her feet. We just forgot what we were doing and acted like we were at an arcade or something."

"We're sorry," echoed Nicole and Ben.

Sam spoke up. "We won't do it again."

"I hope you are both okay," said Bobby.

"We are fine, but you kids need to be more careful. When you are in the clubhouse, you need to act like ladies and gentlemen," said Mrs. Goldman. "This is not the place to run around like wild animals."

Back downstairs, Mike was waiting for them.

"Coach Mike, why did you want to talk about Connecticut?" asked Ben. "I don't know what that has to do with anything."

"It's etiquette, not Connecticut," said Mike. "And it is about how to act appropriately. Who has been to a football game?"

"I have," replied Ben.

"How do the fans act?"

"They scream, shout, throw things, and go crazy," said Ben.

"Why don't golf fans do that?" asked Mike.

"That's easy," interjected Nicole. "That would bother the golfers and affect the game."

Mike continued. "Right. That behavior is not appropriate for golf fans, and they would be escorted off the course. If you were at home with a bunch of friends, would it be okay to run around like wild animals?"

"Well, maybe," said Sam. "But only outside. My mom would never allow us to do that inside."

"Right again," said Mike. "So, some types of behavior are okay in some places but not in others."

"I think we get it, Coach Mike," said Bobby.

"Okay, then. What about on the golf course? Is it okay to step on the line of someone's putt?"

"No."

"What about throwing your club if you hit a bad shot?"

"Definitely not okay."

"What about slamming your club into the ground in anger?"

"No way. That is wrong and it also hurts the golf course."

"What about using bad language?"

"Any of those things could get us disqualified from a tournament."

"Is it okay to talk while someone is playing ping-pong?"

"Sure, we do it all the time."

"What about when someone is hitting a shot on the golf course?"

"No, that wouldn't be good."

"What about walking ahead of someone before they hit their shot, or standing in their line and distracting them?"

"All of those things are bad on the golf course," said Ben. "But some of them may be okay in other places."

"Ah, that is the point of etiquette," said Mike. "Etiquette is like an unwritten set of rules that tells you how to act in different situations. What is right in one place might not be right in another."

Isabella jumped in. "So as golfers, we need to know how to act on the course, and in the clubhouse."

"Right. If you are going to be a golfer, you need to act like one. That means respecting the game, the golf course, the other players, and yourselves."

"Does respecting the game mean to honor its traditions?" asked Sam.

"Yes," replied Mike. "It means appreciating the beauty of golf, its rich history, and following the rules."

"I'll bet that respecting the golf course means to take care of it. Like raking bunkers, repairing ball marks on the green, and fixing divots," said Nicole.

"Perfect," said Mike.

"And not damaging the grass by slamming my club on the ground." added Bobby.

"What about respecting the other players?" asked Ben. "Does that mean to be quiet when they are hitting and to give them a fair chance to play their best?"

"Yes," said Mike. "Even though you want to win, you want them to do their best too. You need to show good sportsmanship."

"And respecting ourselves means to be true to ourselves and always try to do our best," offered Isabella.

"Right again," said Mike.

"I think we learned our lesson, Coach Mike," they all said together.

CHAPTER SEVEN

"I take pride in myself, and in all my work too. To be the best I can be, and do the best I can do."

– RICK HEARD

ONE STROKE

"Wow," said Isabella after Mike went back upstairs. "That was bad. I feel like we really let Coach Mike down. He's right, we are lucky to be able to use the golf course and clubhouse. Not many kids have that opportunity. We'll have to be more careful. What would we do if we couldn't come here any more?"

"That would be awful," said Nicole. "Next

time we all need to be more respectful."

They turned their attention to the TV, which was tuned to the Golf Channel. The announcers were discussing the recent PGA Tour event and showing the final leaderboard and money winnings.

"Wow! Look at that. The winner won almost a million dollars!" exclaimed Ben.

Sam let out a low whistle. "And the guy in second place won half a million dollars. But look, after playing 72 holes of golf, they were only one stroke apart."

"Yeah, and look at the rest of the leaderboard. It's the same thing," said Nicole. "Every extra stroke is worth thousands of dollars." She paused for a moment and continued. "You know, after every round, I can always think of lots of ways I could have saved a single stroke."

"That's a little too late, isn't it?" asked Isabella. "You should think of ways to save that stroke before losing it."

"What do you mean?"

"Well, if you really take care on each shot, maybe you could save a stroke every now and then. Then you would know you had tried your hardest on each shot. I mean, at least I know that I get careless sometimes and don't really do my best on every shot."

"Coach Mike says that every shot is a work of art," said Bobby. "If we really want to do our best, we should take pride in every shot. He says we should imagine what we want our ball to do, then pretend to see it happen before we swing."

"Like a movie in our brains?" asked Ben.

"Yep. He says that each shot is one stroke, and each one deserves our full attention."

"Well, of course each shot is one stroke," laughed Ben. "Unless it goes into a hazard or something. Then it could be two strokes."

Isabella joined in. "Exactly. And look at how important each stroke is. It can be the difference between winning and finishing second. It can make you miss the cut. It can let ten other players pass you on the leaderboard. One stroke can make a huge difference."

"So how are we supposed to do it?" asked Sam. "I mean, taking pride, imagining our shot, watching movies in our heads, doing our best, and all that stuff. I don't really get it."

"Let's ask Coach Mike," suggested Isabella.

After the clubhouse incident, Mike had gone back upstairs to speak with the ladies group, and was now back in his pro shop office. He looked up to see five faces peering at him through the open doorway.

"Hey, you guys," he said. "What's up?"

Isabella took the lead. "Well, we were just talking about how important each stroke is, and how you said we should take pride in every shot and do our best."

"Right."

"But, we're not really sure we know what that means," she continued. "What do we need to do?"

"Hmmm," murmured Mike. "Let me think." He stood up and paused for a moment, then said "Got it. Meet me on the putting green, and bring your putters."

With puzzled looks on their faces, the five friends turned and walked respectfully to their golf bags, got their putters, and made their way to the putting green.

"All right," said Mike. "Let's have a little competition. Ben, Nicole and I will team up and play Bobby, Sam and Isabella in a one-hole putting match. The format will be alternate shot. Bobby, you guys go first. We'll putt from right here to that hole way over there on the other side of the green. The losers will buy the winners a lemonade. Ready?"

Bobby let Sam putt first, since he was the best at lagging long putts close to the hole. His ball took the break, rolled slightly downhill, and ended up only inches from the hole.

"Great putt, Sam!" exclaimed his teammates.

Ben let out a big sigh. "Great putt, Sam. Now, someone go tap that in before it falls into the hole," he said. "Now we know what our team has to do."

"Okay, our turn," said Mike. "Nicole, you lead off for our team."

Nicole had watched Sam's putt, and learned from how the ball traveled to the hole. She gave it just a bit more break, but hit the putt just a little too hard, leaving the ball about four feet past the cup.

"Good job," congratulated Mike. "Ben, do you want to hit this next putt for us?"

"No, thanks," he said, knowing that four-foot putts were not his strong point. "You knock it in, Coach Mike."

"All right. Here goes."

The five friends were shocked when Mike walked quickly up to the ball and hit it without lining it up or even taking a practice swing. The ball missed by six inches and kept rolling past the hole, stopping farther away than it had been before Mike hit the putt.

"Hey, Coach Mike! What happened?" Ben asked. "I could have done better than that."

"What do you mean?" Mike asked. "I did my best."

"No way. That was not your best. It didn't even look like you tried to make it."

Mike had made his point. "Well, what should I have done differently?"

"First," said Nicole, "you should have taken your time and lined up the putt. You could have asked us what we thought. We are a team, you know. And, you could have taken some practice swings to get a feel for the distance."

"Yeah," said Ben. "You basically wasted a stroke, and it cost us a lemonade!"

"All right, you got me," said Mike. "Relax, I'll buy the lemonades. I did that to show you what it looks like when someone doesn't take pride in their shot, or when they don't try to do their best. The ball might have gone in the hole anyway, but it would have almost been an accident. I didn't appreciate the value of a single stroke, and it cost us the match."

"I might have still missed the putt, even if I had really tried to do my best," Mike continued. "But at least I would have tried. Every stroke is so important that it deserves your full attention and your best effort. And, at the end of the round, no matter how well you play, you need to at least know that you took pride in yourself and gave it your best. There is no worse feeling than knowing that you could have done a better job if only you had tried just a little bit harder."

"So, taking pride means that we are careful and think through what we intend to do before we do it," explained Nicole. "And now I can really see how important it is for me to play smarter."

"And that is how we do our best," said Ben.

"Right," said the others.

CHAPTER EIGHT

*"We learn nothing when everything goes well.
We learn everything when nothing goes well."*
– RICK HEARD

MISTAKES ARE GOOD

Mike returned to his office to finish the day's work. Before going home, he still needed to publish the results of the ladies association event, tally the pro shop sales, and get things ready for tomorrow morning's men's day tournament.

The life of a PGA head golf professional is

a combination of politician, businessman, salesman, entrepreneur, teacher, and mentor. He particularly loved teaching, especially teaching junior golfers, and he always looked forward to working with his five favorite students. Most of all, he was honored to have the chance to mentor them and help them learn the values of golf and life.

The five friends remained on the putting green, aimlessly puttering around. Ben was the first to speak.

"You know, I was really surprised when Coach Mike missed that short putt. I thought pros never made mistakes. I know he kind of did it on purpose, but it just caught me by surprise."

Bobby chimed in. "Yeah, it's kind of crazy to think that even PGA pros hit bad shots like we do. You would think that they are better than that."

"For sure," Sam joined in. "I mean, they practice all the time, don't they?"

"I don't know about that," said Nicole. When was the last time you saw Coach Mike on the range or practicing his short game?"

"Hmmm, now that you mention it, I don't see him practicing too often," Sam replied. "He helps us and other people all of the time, but maybe he doesn't have too much time to practice his own game."

"Then even though he is a really good player, he must make plenty of mistakes," said Nicole.

"Everybody makes mistakes or hits bad shots," said Isabella. "Golf is really hard, and mistakes are just part of the game. In reality, mistakes are good, because they help us see what we need to work on."

"You know," Isabella continued, "if we never made any mistakes, things would be kind of boring. I like the challenge of improving my game so that I make fewer mistakes. But, I also like the challenge of recovering from bad shots when I do make a mistake."

"Now that you mention it, so do I," said Ben. "I mean, I like practicing my favorite shots too, but it is really more fun trying to hit tough shots from the rough, over bunkers, and places like that. And I guess I'd never get the chance to hit them if I was always straight down the fairway and on the green."

"Right," said Isabella. "Mistakes are good because they make us stronger. They teach us how to recover and move on."

"Well, I sure never thought of mistakes being good," said Bobby. "They make me so mad sometimes that I just want to scream."

"And how would that help anything?" Isabella asked. "You could scream and pound your club all you want, but your bad shot is still sitting there waiting for you to hit it. And being mad won't help you with your next shot."

"Well, I just don't want to make any mistakes."

Nicole joined in. "Coach Mike told me that

even the best players make mistakes. He said it is more important how we handle ourselves after making a mistake."

"Right," said Isabella. "We can get mad and scream like Bobby, or we can move on and forget about the bad shots."

"But that is impossible for me to do!" said Bobby. "I just get so mad that I can't see straight, and then I don't even know what happens after that. Except that I keep making bogeys and double-bogeys until I snap out of it. By then it is too late to save my round."

"Well, you had better find a way to get over your mistakes before this weekend's tournament," said Isabella. "But now, I've got to get home. I've had enough for today."

"Me too," the others said together.

"I'm really proud of you, Bobby."

CHAPTER NINE

"Your strongest opponent is yourself."

– Anon.

MAD IS BAD

Wednesday morning arrived with the usual warning. The sound of greens mowers, bunker rakes, and leaf blowers preparing the course for the day's play echoed through the course. Mike arrived at six thirty to finalize the setup for the morning's men's day eight o'clock shotgun start.

Ben, Sam, Nicole, Isabella, and Bobby, each home in their own soft beds, slept in for a change. The golf course was reserved for the men's association until afternoon, and they had agreed to meet after lunch for a nine-hole practice round.

Bobby awoke thinking about yesterday's conversation about mistakes. Why was it so hard for him to accept that he wasn't perfect on the golf course? He knew he wasn't perfect anywhere else.

He could think of lots of examples of mistakes he made in other activities besides golf, and none of those bothered him as much as missing the fairway or three-putting from 40 feet.

He thought of mistakes he made in school. He was a good student, but he often overlooked silly errors on his math work. He made zillions of mistakes in his piano lessons. Last week he had been daydreaming when he mistakenly opened the door to the girl's locker room. What the heck? He had even tripped and fallen right in the middle of the soccer field while running after a loose ball during

P.E., but he had just laughed it off.

If he could accept these, why couldn't he accept mistakes on the golf course? He decided to go to the course to talk with Coach Mike, hoping that he might have a few free minutes while the tournament was going on.

The bad thing about those Tuesday and Wednesday events was that Mike had a lot of preparation and follow-up work to do.

The good thing was that, once the players were out on the course, Mike could usually relax a bit and take care of other business.

Bobby was today's business.

"Hi, Coach. Got a few minutes?" Bobby asked as he walked into the pro shop. He knew that Coach Mike would always make time for him if possible.

"Perfect timing," replied Mike. "I just got everything set for this Friday's scramble, and now I have a break before the men finish. What's up?"

"Coach Mike, I'm ready to get rid of my

anger problem."

"Well, that is great news, Bobby. You know, you've been fighting with yourself for a pretty long time now. What brings you to this decision?"

"I don't know. Something Isabella said yesterday just made me realize that I'm my own worst enemy. I mean, I can play great golf sometimes, but if any little thing goes wrong, I lose it and ruin my round. I don't want to do that anymore, especially with the tournament coming up on Saturday."

"I'm really proud of you, Bobby. This is a big decision, and it is the kind of thing you have to decide to do yourself. No one else can make you do it. So tell me, how do you feel about making mistakes?"

"I hate making them."

"So, you're a perfectionist?"

"I guess so, at least on the golf course. I mean, I make plenty of mistakes in other things and they don't bother me so much. But

I just can't stand to make mistakes out there." He pointed to the golf course.

"You know, Bobby, I've always thought that making mistakes was just a normal part of life. There is nothing wrong with making mistakes, especially with something as difficult as hitting a golf ball. Think about it… it is the hardest game in the world. Even the greatest players say that they may hit only one or two perfect shots in a round, if they are lucky. The rest are all mistakes – some of them not so bad, some of them really bad."

Mike paused for a moment, then continued. "With something as difficult as golf, you know you are going to make mistakes. Lots of them. So why let them bother you?"

"I don't know. Maybe I expect too much."

"You can't be perfect, Bobby. You don't have the skills to hit a ball perfectly every time. No one does."

"I know."

"You don't have control over the golf ball. But you do have control over how you react, and you can be perfect in how you handle yourself."

"How do you mean?"

"Here's an example. Last month I was playing in a PGA Section event, and another pro topped his tee shot into the water hazard in front of the tee."

"No way!"

"Yes way. He was trying to hit some kind of special low shot into the wind, and he just cold topped it. Obviously, he was not too happy, but he didn't show it. He just walked over to his bag, took out another ball, teed it up, took a deep breath, and hit the most beautiful low line drive right down the middle of the fairway. Then, he looked over at me and said 'always hit your second shot first.' We laughed so hard my sides were hurting. Then, when he got to his ball, he hit a screaming 3-wood onto the green and made the putt for a par. It was really an eagle with his second ball. I was impressed."

"Wow. He didn't let that awful shot bother him too much!"

"No he didn't, and he hit a few more bad shots during the round, but he always kept a positive attitude. I think he knew that he was good enough to recover from his mistakes. He knew that mistakes are normal. Everybody makes them. He didn't let them ruin his round."

"I wish I could do that," Bobby said.

"You can, Bobby, but you need to start by making sure your expectations are in line with your abilities."

"What do you mean?"

"I mean this. You are young. You are a very good golfer, but you have only been playing for five or six years. You are going to hit some great shots. And, you are going to make mistakes. You know that. Some of them are going to be little mistakes. Some are going to be big ones. Right?"

"Right."

"Those are your expectations. You can't expect perfect."

"Okay."

"Well, then. You shouldn't get angry at things that you expect to happen."

"Hmmm. I never thought of it that way."

"If you expect those things, then they are normal. They are okay. They are challenges that need to be handled. And, you need to handle those challenges with your best skills. You won't have your best skills when you play with an angry mind."

"Right."

"Remember – you are a very good golfer. You can recover. You can let one bad shot cost you only one stroke. You guys have heard me say it: 'let 1 = 1.' Let one bad shot cost you only one stroke – or less. That is what the pros do. You can do it too."

"I guess you're right."

"Don't guess. You can do it. Just tell yourself that you are not going to let your anger beat you. Take a deep breath and hold it for a moment, then let it out slowly. Wait for yourself to calm down. Then, focus on the challenge of the next shot."

"I think I can do that."

"You can, Bobby. You can't change the past. The mistake happened. But you can change the future. You can put the mistake behind you and move on."

"Thanks, Coach. You're the best."

"Thanks for trusting me to talk about this, Bobby. I think you can go forward with a new approach, and you'll have a lot more fun on the golf course."

"I'm going to do it, and I'll prove it this weekend!" Bobby said, and he headed home for lunch.

Isabella's big bag of tools

CHAPTER TEN

"A hammer is a poor substitute for a screwdriver."

– RICK HEARD

THE RIGHT TOOL

Afternoon came slowly for the others, but it sneaked up on Bobby the way his little sister liked to do. "Surprise!!" she yelled from right behind him, startling him out of his shoes and nearly making him blow lemonade out of his nose.

"Aaaahhh! Why do you do that!? I'm gonna get you one of these days. Uh oh. It's already one o'clock. Thanks for lunch, mom. I promised everyone I'd be at the course at one. Gotta go."

He found Sam and Ben on the range, warming up. Like usual, Sam had some new club he was trying. This one looked way too big for him, since it was a full-sized men's driver.

"Watch this," Sam said. "I can hit this thing a mile."

With that, Sam took a looooong backswing that wrapped his arms around his neck like a rubber band. His downswing began by unwrapping his arms and twisting his body so that he could try to coordinate the giant club into the ball without falling down.

He did hit the ball, but it wasn't pretty, and it definitely didn't go a mile.

Laughing hysterically, Ben said "Wow! That was cool. Let me try."

"You guys are crazy," Bobby said.

Sam watched Ben do the same thing, and

the two boys looked at each other and laughed.

"Guess we need to grow a little before using this club," Sam said.

No sooner had the words left his mouth than they saw Mike approaching in his golf cart, with a huge bag of clubs strapped onto the back. Not far behind him were Nicole and Isabella.

Ben spoke for everyone. "Wow. What are all of those clubs, Coach? You must have one of everything in there."

"Hi guys," said Mike. "My shipment of junior demo clubs came this morning while I was busy with the men's tournament. Do you happen to know of anyone who might be available to help me test these things out?"

Five simultaneous "me's" rang out.

"I also have this cool swing speed radar to help figure out which club is the right one. Who knows how we might decide if a club is the right one?"

Bobby spoke up. "The one that hits the ball the farthest."

"Okay, but how could we determine that without walking out on the range to measure?"

"What about clubhead speed?" asked Ben.

"Right. That is a very important thing, especially for young golfers like you guys. We want you to be able to swing the club fast, and swing your arms and hands quickly too. Often, if a club is too long or too heavy, it might hit the ball far but cause you to swing slowly. Like that big driver you were trying, Sam. It is way too long and heavy for you to handle, and it actually makes you learn to swing slower. And, that can really ruin your swing form."

"I sure don't want to do that," said Sam.

"I know you are still using those cut-down clubs from your dad, but these lighter clubs are just the right size for you, and I'm sure you can swing them faster. Want to give them a try?"

"Definitely," Sam agreed.

The time went by in a flash, as Sam and the others all tried several different club sizes. After about 30 minutes, Sam spoke for the group.

"Pretty cool. My swing speed went up five miles per hour with the lighter and shorter clubs. I'm done with using these big, heavy clubs."

"Now, who can tell me something about using the right clubs?" Mike asked.

Bobby answered first. "It is really important to use clubs that are the right size for you."

"Great," said Mike.

"And you need to use the right club for each shot," said Ben.

"Perfect," Mike agreed. "Now let's talk about the short game for a moment. Who uses their sand wedge for every shot around the green, no matter what the circumstances?"

Everyone looked at Isabella.

"Come on, guys, give me a break!" she said.

"I'm great with my sand wedge, and it is better than any other club for chipping. At least it is for me."

Ben pressured her. "But you said you want to improve your short game. None of the rest of us use our sand wedge all of the time. We all chip with 8-irons, 7-irons, pitching wedges, sand wedges, or putters, depending on the shot. Maybe your short game would improve if you tried other clubs."

Mike smoothed things over. "You know, Isabella, you are a very smart girl. You always seem to have the right response or answer to questions and problems. But, you don't give the same answer all of the time."

"Of course not," she agreed. "You can't solve every problem with the same answer."

"Right. Do you think that might apply to problems around the green? I mean, I know it is possible to use any club to get the job done, but perhaps some clubs are better than others for some shots. What do you think?"

"Well, I never really thought of it like that."

"Some shots require the ball to roll for more of the distance, and some shots are easier if the ball flies in the air for more of the distance. It is your job to know which one is which, and then to figure out which club is the best one to solve that problem. It is a lot harder to use one club for everything, because then you need to learn many different ways to hit the ball. It is much easier to learn only a few ways to hit the ball, and then change clubs to use the right tool for the job. Let's give it a try. Come with me over to the chipping green."

"Okay," they all said.

"All right. Let's play a game I call Clubster. Each of you get your sand wedge, pitching wedge, 9-iron, 8-iron, and 7-iron. Also, you will each need ten range balls. Oh, and as usual, there is a catch."

"Ugh. What's the catch?" Isabella asked.

"No two of you can use the same club at

the same time. In other words, someone uses the sand wedge, someone else uses the pitching wedge, someone else uses the 9-iron, and so on. We'll start from here and chip to that hole over there. You will each get two tries, and we will use only the best of the two shots. The person who gets the ball closest to the hole wins. Got it?"

"Got it," they answered together.

They took turns chipping, and Sam, using his 8-iron, won the first round.

"Now for round two, change clubs by going up to the next higher club," said Mike. "If you were using the 7-iron, change to the 8-iron. If you were using the 8-iron, change to the 9-iron. If you were using the sand wedge, change to the 7-iron. Okay?"

"Got it."

This time, Isabella won using her 9-iron. They continued rotating clubs. Sam won the third round with his pitching wedge; Ben won the fourth round with his 8-iron, and Bobby won the final round, also with his 8-iron. Thinking he had won the game, because he had won two rounds, Sam cheered and gave his best fist pump.

However, Mike surprised them.

"Great job, Sam, for winning twice. But you did not win the game."

"Huh?" they all said.

"Nope. The 8-iron won the game, since it won three times. The sand wedge didn't win any of the rounds."

"Hey, that's not fair. We thought we were trying to see which one of us was the best chipper," said Ben.

Mike explained. "Actually, I wanted to see which club was the best for this type of shot. And what I found was that this shot requires a low-lofted club that helps the ball roll up to the hole. The high-lofted wedges didn't work too well for this shot. What do you think, Isabella?"

"Hmmm," she said. "I see the point. I have

a big bag of tools over there, but I always use the same tool, no matter how different the shot. I think my short game can get much better if I can learn to choose the right tool for the job."

"Exactly," agreed Mike.

"Hey guys," Bobby called. "It's getting late, and I want to play nine holes to practice for Saturday's tournament. Anybody want to play?"

Ben decided he wanted to stay at the range and keep playing around with the demo clubs. "Not me. I'm gonna hang out here for a while, then hit the pool. I'll see you guys tomorrow."

Isabella and Nicole decided they would go straight to the pool. "Nah, we're going to the pool now. See you guys later."

Sam accepted Bobby's offer. "I'm in," he said.

CHAPTER ELEVEN

"Practice with no consequences."
– RICK HEARD

PRACTICING AROUND

As they headed to the first tee for a practice round, Bobby spoke to Sam. "Hey Sam, I need to get home in time for dinner, but I want to get in a good practice round. I don't want to be mean, but could you please try to play faster this time? That way, we could play the practice round scramble game that Coach Mike told me about last week."

Sam, famous for his slow play, wasn't offended. "Okay. Remember it is my 'now' goal to play faster. I don't want to be slow, but I just have a hard time deciding what club to use and how to hit the shot. I don't know how you play so quickly. Could you help me do it?"

Bobby was flattered to be asked for help. "Sure, I'll try. I mean, I don't really know how I do it, but maybe I can help."

He thought for a minute and then added "hey, maybe you can help me too. I'm really trying not to get so mad when I play. You're so calm all of the time. Maybe you can help me with my 'now' goal too. Let's get going."

"I'll do my best. But how do we play this practice round game?" asked Sam.

"It's really simple. Any time you don't like the shot you just hit, you can drop a ball and hit the shot again. Then, you decide which one you like the best and use that one."

"So, it's like taking a mulligan whenever

you want?"

"Exactly. Coach Mike says that it takes the pressure off each shot and lets us see how well we can score when our bad shots don't count. I think it will help me relax and not worry about any my mistakes."

"Hmmm. Maybe it will help me play faster, since I won't be so worried about each shot. I'll be able to just go up and hit it. Let's give it a try."

It didn't take long for Bobby to be tested. He hit a great tee shot on the first hole and didn't even use a mulligan. But then his hook showed its ugly head on his approach shot, ending up well left of the green and in the deep rough. Ready to slam his club, he checked himself, took a deep breath, and hit his mulligan on the green. "This might just work," he thought.

Sam had a harder time breaking his slow play habit, but Bobby kept urging him to "just hit it," and not worry so much about where it went. To his surprise, Sam found himself actually hitting better shots. He used mulligans on each shot on the first three holes, but only needed one on the fourth.

By the fourth hole, Bobby was also much more relaxed, and found himself making good swings on his first attempt and not wanting any mulligans. "Crazy," he said to Sam as they walked off the fourth green. "Since I know I have a second chance, I'm not worried about my first shot and, like magic, I'm playing so much better."

"Me too," said Sam. "I can just go up and hit my ball without thinking too much, and the same magic is working for me."

By the eighth hole, both boys were having a blast and playing what seemed to be easy golf.

"Let's go back to regular golf for the last hole," Sam suggested.

"Okay," Bobby agreed. "No mulligans on this hole. But, I'm going to pretend like I can use one."

"Me too."

Bobby cranked a long, straight tee shot right down the middle of the fairway. "Yes!" he exclaimed. Sam teed his ball, then started to freeze up.

"Come on, buddy," Bobby encouraged. "Just hit it."

He did, and it was his best drive of the day. "All right!" Sam yelled.

As Bobby stood over his approach shot, his mind automatically shifted to thoughts of his nemesis – that hook. With water on the left next to the green, that hole had claimed way too many of Bobby's golf balls. He took his backswing and added one more ball to the lake.

"Arrrrrgh!!" he shouted, and caught himself as he started to slam his club.

"Hey Bobby," Sam interrupted. "Don't worry, you can hit another shot."

"What do you mean," Bobby shot back.

"I'm in the water again."

Sam continued. "Well, think of it like this. You hit your first shot into the water. Now you can drop another and pretend like it is your mulligan."

"Yeah, but this one counts," sighed Bobby.

"Just hit it," said Sam, and Bobby laughed at hearing his own words come back at him.

Bobby dropped a second ball, made a great swing, and sent his ball flying to the green.

"Always hit your second shot first," Sam said, and both boys erupted into laughter.

"You know, you're okay for a little kid," said Bobby.

"And you're okay for a big monster," answered Sam.

"You know, if I can take this attitude to the course on Saturday, I think I will be able to play really well."

"You can do it," Sam said with a smile.

CHAPTER TWELVE

"Every great player is a great putter."
– RICK HEARD

THE PUTTING LESSON

Ben awoke with a start from a Thursday morning dream. Still in a fog and half asleep, he remembered something about a giant golf ball trying to find its way into a tiny hole.

"What's the matter with me?" he thought. "I've got to get over these putting problems. I've been hitting the ball so well, then blowing

Ben's nightmare.

my chances on the greens."

As he lay there, he remembered that Coach Mike held a clinic each Thursday morning, and today's topic was putting. It was already eight o'clock and he had to get moving fast to get there by nine.

Mike had created the weekly clinics to help promote the game of golf, and they were open to everyone including junior golfers. Usually the clinics were full, and today was no exception. Ben arrived just in time to squeeze in. Looking across the green, he saw Isabella.

Mike was just getting started.

"Okay everyone, today we are going to work on our putting. Can anyone tell me why putting is so important?"

Someone asked "because the putter is the club we use for the most shots?"

"Exactly," Mike answered. "Believe it or not, for many golfers, nearly half of all strokes are putts. Even the best golfers use their putter 40 percent of the time. If you really want to improve your scores, you need to improve your putting."

Ben heard a few murmurs of surprise throughout the group. Mike had certainly gotten his attention, too.

"So, since putting is so important, let's all learn how to be a better putter," Mike said. "There are two things that really matter in putting. Who can tell me what they are?"

A woman said "aim."

"Right. We'll call it 'direction.' And what is the second thing?"

Isabella got up the courage to speak. "Distance," she offered.

"Perfect. Thanks, Isabella. By the way, everyone, we are lucky to have Isabella and Ben with us today. They are both outstanding young golfers, and they are both playing in this weekend's tournament."

Ben and Isabella shrank in embarrassment as the rest of the group applauded.

"Okay," continued Mike. "Now, who can

tell me which one of those two things is the most important?"

Several voices shouted out "direction!"

Mike was ready for them. "All right, I have a question for you. Have you ever missed a ten foot putt by five feet to the left or right?" He knew the answer would be "no."

Everyone shook their head as lots of "no's" filled the air.

Mike continued. "No matter how bad you are as a putter, you probably have almost never been that far off with your direction. But what about distance? How many of you have ever hit a ten-foot putt too hard and sent your ball rocketing five feet past the hole?"

Almost everyone laughed as they recalled their own horror stories of ramming putts way past the hole or leaving long putts way short.

Afraid to speak up, Ben thought "Hmmm. I do that all of the time."

Mike went on. "Let's face it. No one likes those testy four to five footers, and that is what happens when our distance control is poor. So, it is really important to be able to make your ball stop near the hole. Here are a few things we can do to help control our putting distance."

"First, your putting stroke should be made using your big muscles like your arms and shoulders. Our wrists and hands give us power that we don't need or want when putting. Your putting stroke should look something like a pendulum."

"What's a pennalam?" Ben asked.

Everyone laughed.

"It's 'pendulum,' Ben, like the thing that swings on a grandfather clock.

"Oh, yeah. We have one of those," Ben said, his face flushed red with embarrassment.

"Your arms and putter should swing together like a pendulum," Mike continued. "And the length of your backswing should control the distance your ball will roll. Ben, does the pendulum in your grandfather clock swing the same distance on each side?"

Afraid to speak again, Ben nodded in agreement.

"And that is important in putting, too. Your putter should follow through at least as far as the backswing."

Mike then showed the group some distance control practice games they could play. Ben's favorite was Sneak Attack, where you have to hit as many putts as you can so that each putt comes as close as possible to the one before it, without touching or going past. Mike called it "Sneak Attack" because each ball must sneak up on the prior ball.

"Now, what about direction?" Mike asked the group. "Even though distance control is number one, direction is really important too, especially for shorter putts. Direction has two parts. The first is knowing where to aim, or reading the greens and figuring out how much your ball will curve, or break. Reading greens is an art that takes lots of experience and practice, but if you look carefully, you can see the slope of the green and know which way the putt will break. Who can guess the second part?"

Isabella gathered her courage and said "actually hitting your ball where you want to aim?"

"Exactly right," Mike congratulated her as everyone applauded again. "Once you figure out where to aim your putt, you have to be able to actually hit it on that line. It sounds easy, but it is an important skill. Watch and I'll show you a very simple way to test your ball-rolling skill."

With that, Mike took a range ball with a thick black stripe around it and placed it on the green with the stripe aligned straight up and down. Then, he lined up his putter with the stripe on the ball.

"Okay, now I'm going to hit this ball with my putter face slightly open." As he did, the ball came off spinning sideways. Everyone gasped.

"There's no way that ball would roll in the right direction," someone said.

"Right," said Mike. "With that sidespin, the ball won't stay on line. Now, watch this."

Mike aligned the ball and his putter again, then made a perfect stroke, keeping his putter face square. As the ball rolled, the stripe stayed perfectly lined up.

"Whew," he said. "I'm always afraid I might spin that one too. As you can see, that putt rolled true in the direction I was aiming. Now let's see you all try it," and he handed each person a striped range ball.

Ben was amazed at how hard it was to just roll the ball without the stripe spinning sideways. "This just might be my biggest problem with short putts," he thought.

As the clinic ended and the group wandered away, Ben and Isabella remained on the green.

"That was amazing," Isabella said.

Ben agreed. "Yeah. I think I know what I need to work on to stop leaving myself those five-footers for par."

"And to start making those five-footers for birdies," Isabella said.

CHAPTER THIRTEEN

"There is no telling how many miles you will have to run while chasing a dream."

– Anon.

HANG IN THERE

After the putting clinic, Ben was frustrated. "Why can't I roll five balls in a row without spinning the stripe sideways?" he wondered. Often, when something was difficult, he would simply avoid doing it or find some excuse to do something else.

Today, he decided, would be different.

With the tournament coming up in only two days, he knew he needed to figure this out.

"I can't let this beat me!" he said to himself. He decided to keep trying and not leave the green until he did five in a row.

He started over and rolled the first ball perfectly. For as long as he could remember, this was the first time he had really focused on something and practiced it.

He knew that his friends didn't mind working on the difficult parts of their game, and he wondered why it was so hard for him to do that. He did want to improve. He just didn't really want to work at it. Until now.

He rolled the second ball perfectly.

Isabella had remained at the practice green also, and was now chipping with her 8-iron. Ben was so lost in his own thoughts that he didn't even notice that Nicole and Sam had shown up.

Sam went over to Ben. "Hey, Ben. What's up with the range ball? Did you lose all of your golf balls? I've never seen you putt with one of those before."

"Arrgh!" Ben shouted as he spun the next ball like a top. "I almost had three in a row! I'm doing this putting drill that Coach Mike showed us in the clinic. It's really hard for me to do it. Here, I'll show you. I'd like to see what you can do."

Ben showed Sam how to align the ball, then watched in amazement as Sam hit putt after putt, each one with the stripe rolling perfectly upright. He stopped at twelve in a row.

"Is this how it is supposed to work?" teased Sam.

"That is unbelievable. It's incredible. How do you do that? I have a hard time doing five in a row, and you just did twelve. I bet you could keep going forever."

Sam thought for a moment, then replied. "You know, I used to have a real hard time with those short putts. It bothered me that something so mechanical like putting could be so hard for me. So I practiced at home until I

Sam rolling the stripe.

could make 100 putts in a row on our putting mat. It was hard work, but I stuck with it."

"So that's why you are such a good putter," Ben said. He started over and spun the first ball. "Man, I don't think that I have ever practiced anything that much."

"Well, maybe that is why this is hard for you. You need to keep trying until you figure it out. Coach Mike calls it 'perseverance,' or hanging in there. You know how important these putts are. It is worth the effort."

Ben started over again and rolled the first ball perfectly.

Isabella overheard the conversation and came over. "What did you say about Percy V's aunts?"

Ben's second ball was perfect.

Sam and Ben looked at each other and said "Huh?"

Ben figured it out. "Oh, you mean 'perseverance.' It means don't quit." He hung his head. "I guess I didn't realize it, but that is what I've been doing. I try a few short putts, then when I miss them I give up and go practice something else."

Ben's third ball showed nothing but the stripe. He started to feel nervous.

"Wow. I think I do the same thing," said Isabella. "I don't like trying these different clubs for chipping. I just want to keep using my sand wedge for every shot."

Sam joined in again. "Coach Mike says that quitters never win, and winners never quit. If something is worth doing, you need to keep trying and never give up."

Ben's fourth ball was perfect. One more to go. Now he *was* nervous.

"Hey, he told me the same thing a while ago," said Isabella. "I just forgot."

Ben took a deep breath and focused all of his energy and prepared to roll his next putt.

"I know we always play practice games with each other, and they are a lot of fun," Sam said. "But sometimes, I think we each need to just find one thing to work on and practice it until we get it. It can get boring, but it isn't that hard to do. It just takes perseverance."

Punching the air and letting out a primal scream, Ben yelled "Yeah! Five in a row! Let's see if I can get to ten…"

CHAPTER FOURTEEN

"Someone is always watching you, so be a great role model."

– RICK HEARD

ROLE MODELS

After lunch, Ben and Sam decided to take a break and hang out at the pool for a while. "Maybe Bobby will come by and hang out with us too," Ben said. He would never admit it, but he loved being around the older kids, especially Bobby. And Bobby never realized how much of a role model he had become for Ben.

Ben looked up to the others, too, and had come to appreciate their strengths. Bobby was big and strong, and could hit the golf ball almost out of sight. It was even a good thing that Ben had seen the darker side of Bobby's temper. "I don't want to act like that," he had decided one day a few months ago when Bobby had embarrassed himself in front of the world.

Ben and Bobby had been out for a fun nine holes. Bobby had missed the green on the third hole, then hit a nice pitch shot up to about eight feet from the hole. Then, disaster had struck.

What could have been a nice par, had he made the putt, turned into a three-putt for a double-bogey. Bobby had shouted and stomped around on the green, then slammed his putter on the ground.

Unfortunately for Bobby, Coach Mike and several adults had been watching from the nearby practice green. His dad had even witnessed the entire show from the pro shop window!

That had been the last straw. Mike had come over and demanded that Bobby apologize to everyone. Then, Mike got Bobby a job for the week working with the greens crew, fixing divots, raking bunkers, and repairing every little bad spot of grass he could find. Worst of all, his dad had parked Bobby's clubs in the garage for the week.

That was all that Ben had needed to see. He promised himself that he would never act like that. Still, Ben admired Bobby and wanted more than anything to be able to hit the golf ball like Bobby could.

He also wished he had Sam's patience and ability to think things through. He really admired Sam's putting skills. Just seeing what Sam had done rolling the stripe was enough to encourage Ben to practice a little harder and keep trying.

Ben hated to admit it, but he also admired

the girls. Nicole had a reckless flair to her golf game, and she never backed down. Ben had seen her pull off some amazing shots that no one else would have ever even tried.

Of course, he had also seen her waste many nice rounds by going for broke when she should have played it safe. One day she had come to the eighteenth hole needing a par for a 79. It would have been her best round ever. Instead of hitting a five wood off the tee, she tried to cut the corner of the dogleg with her driver and ended up in the rough.

Ben cringed as he remembered what had happened next. "Chip out to the fairway," he had suggested when he saw where her ball was. But "play safe" was not a part of Nicole's vocabulary.

She had taken her hybrid and aimed at a small opening between the trees and fired at the green, hoping to get on in two and have a birdie putt. After three attempts, her ball bouncing off the trees like a pinball game, she had finally chipped out to safety. By the time she had putted out, her needed par had turned into an unwanted double-par, and her 79 into an 83.

Seeing that had helped Ben appreciate the balance between being aggressive and playing smart. "There is a time for taking risks, and a time to play safe," he told himself. "I just need to know which is which."

Of all of his friends, Isabella seemed to be the one who put all of the pieces together. She had a solid game and although she was not a long hitter, she rarely mis-hit a shot. More than anything, she seemed to know her strengths and she played to them.

Once, Isabella had hit a perfect tee shot, leaving her in reach of the green on the 15th hole, a par five. Ben had been surprised that she hadn't gone for the green. Instead, she had taken a 6-iron and laid up, leaving her ball about 40 yards from the hole.

"Why did you do that?" he had asked her.

"I would have gone for it."

"Well," she had replied. "There are bunkers and deep grass around the green, and I would have had to hit a perfect five wood to reach. Even if I had landed my ball on the green, it might have rolled off into the deep stuff. I'm not that good from those spots around the green, but I am deadly from 40 yards. That is my favorite shot, so I put my ball there for the best chance to make a birdie."

Ben had never thought about golf like that until hearing Isabella's explanation and then watching her stick her sand wedge to five feet and drain the birdie putt.

Lying beside the pool with the hot sun blazing, Ben thought of how he could use the best pieces of each of his friends to shape his own approach. Strong like Bobby. Patient like Sam. Aggressive like Nicole. Smart like Isabella. And confident like himself. If he could do that, his golf game would change forever.

CHAPTER FIFTEEN

"To really understand your own game, walk nine holes in someone else's golf shoes."

– RICK HEARD

ROLE REVERSAL

While Ben and Sam were at the pool and Bobby was who-knows-where, Isabella and Nicole went out to play nine holes. They didn't usually get to play together without the boys joining in. A girls-only nine was nice for a change.

"What should we do?" Nicole asked Isabella. "Do you want to play regular stroke play or match play today?"

"I have an idea," said Isabella. "I've never done this before, but let's try it. I'll caddy for you and you caddy for me."

"What do you mean?"

"Well, you said you want to play more cautiously like me, and I'd like to be more aggressive like you sometimes. So I'll tell you what type of shot to hit and you tell me what type of shot to hit. I promise I'll do whatever you suggest. And I'll only tell you to do what I would really do if I were hitting your ball."

"Cool. I promise I'll do the same. It sounds like fun."

It didn't take long for Nicole to experience Isabella's different approach. After hitting a good drive down the right side of the first fairway, Nicole wanted to go for the green in two. She wouldn't have minded if her shot had landed in the hazard to the right of the green, but Isabella wouldn't have tried that shot.

"Here you go," said Isabella as she handed Nicole her hybrid. "Hit your hybrid to the safe area short and left of the green," she advised. Nicole obeyed, but pushed her shot to the right and into the light rough bordering the greenside bunker.

"See there," said Isabella. "If you had hit that shot toward the green, you would have gone into the hazard. But now you have an easy pitch shot and a great chance for a birdie, instead of struggling to make a par."

Nicole wasn't totally convinced. "Maybe I wouldn't have pushed my shot if I had gone for the green," she thought.

When Nicole mentioned her doubts, Isabella said "Well, think of it like this. If you had a bucket of 50 range balls and went for the green from here with all of them, how many would you have hit on the green?"

Nicole thought for a moment, then said "Maybe 20 of them."

"So, let's assume you would two-putt each of those for birdie. What about the other 30 shots?"

"I guess about 20 of them would have been in the hazard, and the other 10 in the bunker or in the deep grass around the green."

"Okay. Let's assume that you would hit good bunker shots and pitch shots onto the green and two-putt for par on those 10 balls. But, the 20 balls in the hazard would be worse. Let's assume you would make 10 bogeys and 10 double-bogeys on those. Sound fair?"

"Sure."

"So, that means you would be 10 over par for those 50 balls."

"Hmmm. Interesting."

"Now, let's take the same basket of 50 balls and play them the way I suggested. How many would you hit safely to the lay-up area?"

"Well, that shot is pretty easy, so I think I would hit 40 of them to that area. I guess the other 10 would be in the bunker or in the rough. I'd never hit any of them into the hazard."

"Okay. Now, let's assume that you would

pitch onto the green with the 40 balls. Fair enough?"

"Sure."

"And you would make a birdie with 10 of those 40 and two-putt the rest for par. Good so far?"

"Uh, sure. I think I would make at least ten birdies from there."

"And you would pitch onto the green or hit on from the bunker with the other 10 and make par. Fair enough?"

"Sure. So what does all of this mean?"

"It means that you would be 10 under par for those 50 balls hit to the layup area, compared with 10 over for the risky go for the green shot."

"Wow! That is amazing. Now I see what you are talking about. I should go for shots where my chances of success are high and the penalty for missing is low."

"Exactly!"

Isabella got a taste of Nicole's approach on

the first hole too. After hitting into the fairway bunker on the left side, she normally would have blasted out safely with a wedge, leaving a longer shot to the green but ensuring she escaped from the bunker. Nicole had a different idea.

"Okay," Nicole said. "You are a great iron player, right? And your ball is sitting up nicely in the sand. So, take your 5-iron, grip down a bit, play the ball back in your stance, and rip it toward the layup area short and left of the green, where you told me to go."

Isabella hit the shot a bit thin, but it bounced and rolled right to the center of the layup area. "I guess that is an example of a good place to take a risk. I would have played too safe and had a difficult third shot to the green. I bet I would make par or birdie most of the time using your approach."

"So sometimes my go for broke strategy is good?" Nicole asked.

"Definitely. And sometimes my cautious strategy is good," agreed Isabella.

CHAPTER SIXTEEN

*"**T**ogether **E**veryone **A**chieves **M**ore."*

– Anon.

THE TEAM

Meanwhile at the pool, Bobby wandered in while Sam and Ben were taking an afternoon nap in the poolside lounge chairs. Spying his prey like the king of the jungle, he snuck quietly through the maze of chairs to the edge of the pool. Gathering his strength, he leaped into the pool, spun around in mid-air, and landed a perfect cannonball. A huge plume of water launched over the edge and landed with an enormous splash right on the backs of the two boys.

"Ahhhhh!" Sam and Ben shouted together as the cool water steamed off of their hot skin. When the shock of their surprise shower had gone away, Sam spoke first. Not wanting to give Bobby the satisfaction of winning the battle, he said "Thanks a lot, Bobby. That was really quite refreshing! Would you please splash me again, but this time on the other side?"

With that, the three boys all jumped into the pool and had a good old-fashioned water fight. By the time the lifeguard finally blew the whistle, the boys were exhausted.

"All right, all right. That's enough," said Ben. I'm the little guy here, remember? Where were you all morning, Bobby?"

"Oh, I had to go back to the orthodontist to fix another broken wire. Believe your mom when she says not to eat chewy candy bars when you have braces."

"Sounds like your mom is always right, Bobby," Sam teased.

"Yeah, she probably is, but I never admit it," Bobby replied. "What have you guys been doing all day?"

Ben answered. "Well, Isabella and I went to Coach Mike's putting clinic, then Sam and I putted for a while, then we crashed here after lunch while Nicole and Isabella went out for nine holes after lunch. Whew! That was a mouthful!"

"Well, I want to go hit a few balls," said Bobby. "You guys want to hit the range?"

"Okay," said Sam. "But first, I need to talk to Ben."

"About what?" asked Ben.

"Well, you know I didn't sign up for the tournament. I wasn't feeling too great about my game last week. But now, I really wish I had signed up. I'm using those demo junior clubs, and I'm hitting the ball so much better. But, it's too late to sign up. So, I'd like to caddy for you. If you don't mind, that is."

Ben was surprised, flattered, and embarrassed, all at the same time. "Wow, Sam" he stammered. "I, ah, I would be honored to have you caddy for me. I mean, you are so calm and thoughtful, and you are such a great putter, that I know you would be a big help to me."

"That's teamwork," Sam said. "Together everyone achieves more."

Now, let's go to the range with Bobby and you can figure out my yardages and stuff," said Ben.

CHAPTER SEVENTEEN

"Your body is ready. Prepare your mind."
– RICK HEARD

READY

Friday arrived with a thick, heavy dew that soaked their shoes before they reached their tee shots on the first hole. The morning sun made the fairways look like they were covered with a blanket of diamonds, and their golf balls left long trails in the wet grass. Just one day until the tournament and they were almost ready. Today was a day for a relaxed practice round.

Ben and Bobby went out first, with Sam on

Ben's bag. Nicole and Isabella followed, this time making their own club choices and strategy decisions. They had learned so much from each other yesterday. And, they had Coach Mike's advice from this morning still fresh in their minds.

As usual, Mike had arrived early, and the five friends had been waiting for him in the pro shop. They had many questions. As usual, Mike had answers.

"Coach Mike, since I'm not playing in the tournament, I decided to caddy for Ben," Sam had said, searching for advice on how he could be of the most help. "How do you get ready for a tournament?"

"Great question, Sam," Mike had replied. "First, I make sure I know my tee time and where the golf course is. I know that won't be a problem for you guys, since it is here at your home course. Before the event, I practice from the tournament yardages so I know what clubs I will use on each hole. Usually, the course is marked the day before the tournament, with spray-painted marks on each tee box showing all of the tee marker locations."

"Wow. I never knew that."

"And the hole locations are also marked with a spray-painted dot on each green. When I play a final practice round, I don't putt to the actual hole. Once I reach the green, I putt to the painted dot from several different angles so I can learn the breaks around where the hole will be."

"In between, I don't worry about my swing or my shots. I just play for fun, and move my ball to where I'd like it to be. Sometimes that is in the rough, so I can be ready for the thick grass. Other times that may be in the fairway, where I hope to be in the tournament. Whenever I can, I practice shots around the green, from bunkers and pitch or chip shots."

"My main goal is to come away from my practice round with positive thoughts and good memories. I never keep score, and I hit extra shots whenever I feel like it."

"The only other thing is to not get too tired. It is tempting to play or practice too much before a tournament. You want to be strong and fresh, not tired and sore. Play one round, and then take it easy. Putt for a while, then get a good dinner and a good night's sleep."

"Coach Mike," Sam had asked, "what do I need to do to be a great caddy?"

"Well, Sam, a great caddy is first a great teammate. You and Ben will be partners, and your job will be to help him play his best. You'll carry his clubs. You'll measure the yardages and give him the facts. When he needs it, you'll help him select the right club, but your job is to be his advisor. He is the one who will have to decide what to do, because he will have to live with the outcome."

Mike continued. "You may have to take the blame for a bad shot or two, so go ahead and do it. Make him feel like he is the best golfer in the world, and that any mistakes might just be partly your fault too. Most of all, don't say anything when he does hit a bad shot. He will know it is bad, so you don't have to rub it in. Just hustle to the ball and get ready with your best advice for the next shot."

"Wow, I'd like to have a caddy like that," said Isabella.

"Yeah, but it is also nice to be able to handle things ourselves," added Nicole.

Ben agreed. "It's great to be able to play by myself, but it's also really nice to have a teammate like Sam to help."

"Well, you are lucky to have such a great friend, Ben," said Mike. "Any more questions?"

"Just one," said Bobby. How do you handle being nervous? I get pretty worked up on the first tee sometimes, and then I don't play my best right from the start."

"Being nervous is a good thing," Mike had replied. "It shows that you care and that you are pumped up for the event. I try to remember that I have a long day ahead, and that my first shot will be only one shot of many. That first tee shot is important, but it doesn't count any more than a one-inch putt. That helps me keep it in perspective and relax, so I can make my best swing on the first tee."

"Most important, I always stick to my pre-shot routine. That way, I can focus on each shot and block out the distractions and interference. That is why I showed you guys how to create your own pre-shot routine. Use it on each shot, no matter what. And most of all, remember to have fun. You will play your best when you enjoy yourselves and don't worry about your scores."

"Coach Mike, you are the best," Ben had said. Everyone agreed, and they had headed to the first tee.

When they finished their rounds, they were as ready as they could be. The only thing left to do was relax by the pool and wait.

CHAPTER EIGHTEEN

"Your finish is the result of your preparation."

– RICK HEARD

TOURNAMENT TIME!

Ben had gone out early, with Sam on the bag. He hadn't known either of his two fellow competitors, but they were nice players. Each of them had their dad as a caddy.

Sam almost didn't recognize Ben. His game was sharp and his attitude was like that of a tour pro. Ben's thoughts from the pool yesterday had transformed his game. He had somehow been able to blend the best characteristics of his friends and bring out his best when it counted.

He carded a 2-under par 34.

There was nothing to do but wait and see how the other players did. No matter what, Ben knew he had done his best.

"Sam, thanks for helping me today," Ben said, as they sat on the hillside behind the ninth green watching the other players come in. "You were a huge help, especially with reading the greens and getting my putting speed right."

"Well, you know that is my strength," said Sam. "But you were amazing. I know we have played together many times, but I've never seen you like this. You really saved your best for today."

"Thanks. Hey look," Ben called. "Here comes Nicole. And Isabella is in the group right behind her. And I think Bobby is only a couple of groups behind them. Let's watch them finish."

Nicole had driven her ball into the right rough, and had a tricky shot to the green. With water all along the left side of the fairway and green, and the hole tucked close to the left side, she had a risky approach.

The boys were surprised to see Nicole aim for the right front of the green, ensuring a safe approach and, at worst, a bogey. She hit a perfect safe shot and two-putted for a par, carding a great round of 39. After she signed her card, she joined Ben and Sam behind the green.

"Way to finish, Nicole," Sam said. "But why didn't you go for the flag on that approach like you always do?"

"I played smart," she said. "I had a great round going, and I wanted to make sure I didn't make a big mistake. I think I learned a lesson or two this week."

"Me too," said Ben. "My putting was much better, and it really helped to have Sam's help."

As they chatted, Isabella came into view. She had hit an aggressive tee shot down the left side, leaving a mid-iron to the green. Nicole, Sam, and Ben cringed as they watched her approach shot come up short. "Bet she will try to chip with her sand wedge," Ben said.

"I don't know," said Nicole. "I hope she hits a bump and run or putts it or something. That is a difficult spot for a sand wedge."

They watched as Isabella pondered her situation. She needed to get up and in for par to shoot a 40. Another girl in her group was on the green with a short birdie putt that would also give her a 40. Nicole could see Isabella take a deep breath and reach for her 8-iron. "Good!" she sighed.

Isabella's chip carried a few feet up the slope, took the break and rolled like a putt, curving and slowing perfectly until it disappeared into the hole.

"Yes!" Isabella shouted.

"Yes!" her friends screamed.

When she had signed her card, Isabella joined her friends to watch Bobby finish.

"How did you play?" she asked Ben and Nicole at the same time. "I had a great round, thanks to you, Nicole. And thanks to Coach Mike for the chipping lesson!"

"I shot a 39 too," answered Nicole. "And, thanks to you, I played smart and only made one big mistake. I think it was my best round ever."

"I played great, too," said Ben. "I tried to swing like Bobby, go for it like Nicole, putt like Sam, and think like you."

"Speaking of Bobby, here he comes," said Isabella. "And don't look now, but he is close to the hazard on the left side of the fairway."

"Uh oh," remembered Sam. "A couple of days ago he was near there and hooked his approach into the water."

Ben, Sam, Nicole, and Isabella stood to

watch their friend hit his approach shot. "Come on, Bobby. You can do it," Ben said to himself.

Out in the fairway, Bobby surveyed his situation and thought about his round so far. Like usual, he had been nervous on the first tee. Unlike usual, Coach Mike's words still echoed in his head, and he knew that his tee shot was only one of many shots he was going to hit today. He had striped it right down the center of the fairway.

In spite of another three-putt on the third hole, he had kept his temper under control. He knew he probably wasn't going to win, but he was playing well and hadn't hit any big hooks until his approach shot into the bunker on the eighth hole. He had almost lost his temper then, but somehow he had kept it together, remembering Coach Mike's advice.

"You're good enough to recover from mistakes," Coach Mike had said, and he had been right. Bobby had escaped from the bunker and saved his par. But, another hook here into the hazard would be disastrous.

Then he heard his own words to Sam as he said to himself "Just hit it, Bobby." That brought him back to the present.

He had a good lie and a clear shot to the green. But there was that water! The same lake he had filled with golf balls all summer. The same lake he had hooked his ball into on Wednesday. He tried to block those thoughts from his mind, but it was difficult.

"What do I do?" he asked himself, and then again he recalled Coach Mike's advice. "Take a deep breath and imagine your ball flying as you want it to fly and landing where you want it to land. And always use your pre-shot routine to focus on the shot."

Bobby took a deep breath, pulled his seven-iron from his bag, and took a practice swing. He saw his target, a few yards to the right of the hole and safely away from the water. He played a movie of the shot in his mind and saw his ball flying to the green, then spinning left towards the hole. He took his stance and looked at the target one final time.

And then, he hit his second shot first.

Five golf friends.

About the Author

Rick Heard is a PGA teaching professional and co-owner of the Don Law Golf Academy in Boca Raton, Florida. The academy specializes in teaching juniors, and has hundreds of junior golfers in its classes and camps in four South Florida locations.

Rick is also the author of "Daddy Caddy on the Bag," a book aimed to help parents coach and develop their children's golf games.

He is a co-founder and partner with ParKit Golf, which creates innovative teaching tools and materials to make junior golf classes and camps both fun and educational. Rick was president of the Southeast Chapter of the South Florida Section PGA for six years ending in 2012, and was awarded the chapter's Golf Professional of the Year award for 2010.

He resides in Boca Raton, Florida with his wife Diane and their son Alex.

Made in the USA
San Bernardino, CA
13 March 2016